Chapter 1: Introduction to Arti cial Intelligence

What is Arti cial Intelligence?

Arti cial Intelligence, commonly referred to as AI, represents a branch of computer science that aims to create machines capable of performing tasks that typically require human intelligence. These tasks include learning, reasoning, problem-solving, perception, language understanding, and even social interaction. The concept of AI has evolved signi cantly since its inception, transitioning from theoretical discussions in academic circles to practical applications that permeate various aspects of daily life. Today, AI is not merely a futuristic idea but a present-day reality that in uences industries, economies, and personal experiences.

At its core, AI can be categorized into two main types: narrow AI and general AI. Narrow AI, also known as weak AI,
refers to systems designed to perform speci c tasks, such as voice recognition, image classi cation, or playing chess. These systems operate within prede ned parameters and excel in their designated areas, but they lack the ability to generalize knowledge beyond their speci c functions. In contrast, general AI, or strong AI, represents a hypothetical form of intelligence that possesses the ability to understand, learn, and apply knowledge across a wide range of tasks, similar to human cognitive abilities. While general AI remains largely theoretical, advancements in narrow AI
continue to shape the technological landscape.

The development of AI technologies relies heavily on a variety of techniques and methodologies. Machine learning, a subset of AI, has gained signi cant attention and has become a driving force behind many AI applications. This approach enables systems to learn from data, identify patterns, and make decisions with minimal human intervention. Deep learning, a further subset of machine learning, employs neural networks to analyze vast amounts of data, mimicking the way the human brain processes information. These techniques have led to breakthroughs in areas such as natural language processing, computer vision, and autonomous systems, showcasing the vast potential of AI.

AI's impact is evident across numerous sectors, including healthcare, nance, transportation, and entertainment. In healthcare, AI algorithms assist in diagnosing diseases, personalizing treatment plans, and predicting patient outcomes, ultimately enhancing the quality of care. In nance, AI systems analyze market trends and optimize trading strategies, providing investors with valuable insights. The transportation industry is witnessing the rise of autonomous vehicles, which rely on AI to navigate complex environments safely. As AI continues to evolve, its in uence on various industries will likely expand, creating new opportunities and challenges.

Despite its many bene ts, the rise of AI also raises important ethical and societal considerations. Issues such as job displacement, data privacy, and algorithmic bias demand careful examination and thoughtful responses. As AI systems become more integrated into society, it is crucial to establish guidelines and regulations that ensure responsible development and deployment. By fostering an inclusive dialogue among stakeholders, including technologists, policymakers, and the public, society can harness the power of AI while mitigating its potential risks, paving the way for a future where technology serves humanity's best interests.

Brief History of AI

The history of arti cial intelligence (AI) can be traced back to ancient myths and philosophical inquiries, where the concept of intelligent beings created by humans was rst imagined. Early examples include the Greek myth of Talos, a giant automaton made of bronze, and the philosophical works of gures like Aristotle, who pondered the nature of human thought and reasoning. However, the formal study of AI began in the mid-20th century when computer scientists started exploring the idea of creating machines that could simulate human intelligence.

In 1956, the Dartmouth Conference marked a pivotal moment in AI history. Organized by John McCarthy, Marvin Minsky, Nathaniel Rochester, and Claude Shannon, this event is considered the birth of AI as a eld of research. The attendees proposed that every aspect of learning or any other feature of intelligence could in principle be so precisely described that a machine could be made to simulate it. This led to the development of early AI programs, such as the Logic Theorist and General Problem Solver, which demonstrated that machines could solve problems and make deductions.

The following decades saw both signi cant advancements and setbacks in AI research, commonly referred to as "AI winters." During the 1970s and 1980s, funding and interest in AI waned due to overly optimistic predictions that did not materialize. Researchers faced challenges in creating systems that could understand and process natural language or exhibit common sense reasoning. Nevertheless, contributions from various elds, including cognitive science and neuroscience, continued to shape AI development, leading to improved algorithms and techniques.

The resurgence of AI in the 21st century can be attributed to several key factors, including the exponential growth of computational power, the availability of vast amounts of data, and advancements in machine learning, particularly deep learning. Breakthroughs in neural networks and algorithms have enabled AI systems to perform tasks that were previously thought to be the exclusive domain of humans, such as image and speech recognition, language translation, and complex decision-making. This new era of AI, often referred to as "narrow AI," has led to practical applications across various industries, from healthcare to nance.

As AI continues to evolve, the ethical implications of its use have come into focus. Issues surrounding privacy, bias, and the potential for job displacement have sparked debates among researchers, policymakers, and the public. Understanding the brief history of AI is crucial for grasping its current capabilities and future potential. By re ecting on the past, society can better navigate the challenges and opportunities that AI presents, ensuring that its development aligns with human values and serves the common good.

Importance of AI in Today's World

Arti cial Intelligence (AI) has become an integral part of contemporary society, reshaping various aspects of daily life, industry, and technology. Its signi cance lies not only in its ability to perform complex tasks but also in its capacity to enhance human capabilities and improve decision-making processes. From healthcare to nance, AI systems analyze vast amounts of data, identify patterns, and provide insights that were previously unattainable. This transformative technology is revolutionizing how businesses operate, making them more ef cient and responsive to consumer needs.

In the realm of healthcare, AI plays a critical role in diagnosis and treatment planning. By leveraging machine learning algorithms, medical professionals can analyze patient data and medical histories more effectively, leading to faster and more accurate diagnoses. AI-driven tools assist in predicting disease outbreaks, personalizing treatment plans, and even discovering new drugs. The ability to process and interpret large datasets enables healthcare providers to deliver better patient care while reducing costs, ultimately saving lives and improving health o ut co mes.

The in uence of AI extends into the business sector, where it enhances operational ef ciency and drives innovation. Organizations utilize AI for automating routine tasks, allowing employees to focus on more strategic initiatives. Additionally, AI-powered analytics provide companies with real-time insights into market trends and consumer behavior, enabling them to make data-informed decisions. This competitive advantage is crucial in today's fast-paced environment, where agility and adaptability can determine the success or failure of a business.

AI's impact is also evident in the realm of education, where it personalizes learning experiences for students. Intelligent tutoring systems and adaptive learning platforms cater to individual learning styles and paces, ensuring

that students receive the support they need to succeed. Furthermore, AI aids educators by analyzing student performance data, allowing for targeted interventions and improved teaching strategies. The result is a more inclusive and effective educational landscape that addresses the diverse needs of learners.

However, the rise of AI also brings to light ethical considerations and challenges that society must navigate. Issues such as data privacy, algorithmic bias, and job displacement require careful examination and proactive solutions. As AI continues to evolve, it is crucial for stakeholders—including policymakers, businesses, and the public—to engage in discussions about its implications. By fostering a collaborative approach, society can harness the bene ts of AI while mitigating its risks, ensuring that this powerful technology serves as a force for good in today's world.

Chapter 2: Types of Artificial Intelligence

Narrow AI, often referred to as weak AI, is designed to perform speci c tasks or solve particular problems. This type of arti cial intelligence operates within a limited context and cannot extend its capabilities beyond its programming. For example, voice assistants like Siri and Alexa can understand and respond to voice commands but lack the ability to engage in open-ended conversations or comprehend broader contexts. Narrow AI systems are prevalent in many applications, such as image recognition, recommendation engines, and autonomous vehicles, where they excel in ef ciency and accuracy within their designated domains.

In contrast, General AI, or strong AI, aims to replicate the cognitive functions of the human mind, enabling machines to understand, learn, adapt, and apply knowledge across a wide array of tasks. Unlike narrow AI, which is con ned to speci c tasks, General AI would possess the ability to reason, solve complex problems, and exhibit emotional intelligence. While General AI remains largely theoretical and has not yet been achieved, it is a signi cant focus of research in the AI community and represents the ultimate goal of arti cial intelligence development.

The distinction between narrow and general AI has profound implications for society. Narrow AI, with its current capabilities, is transforming industries by automating repetitive tasks, improving decision-making processes, and enhancing customer experiences. However, the limitations of narrow AI also raise concerns regarding job displacement and ethical considerations in decision-making. In contrast, the realization of General AI could lead to even more signi cant societal changes, potentially altering the workforce landscape, rede ning human-machine interactions, and raising complex ethical dilemmas regarding autonomy and control.

Understanding the differences between narrow and general AI is crucial for fostering informed discussions about the future of technology. As narrow AI continues to permeate various aspects of daily life, awareness of its limitations is essential for setting realistic expectations. Conversely, the prospect of General AI invites speculation about its potential bene ts and risks, encouraging stakeholders to engage in thoughtful discourse about the ethical and societal implications of such advancements.

The journey from narrow to general AI is fraught with challenges, including technical hurdles, ethical considerations, and the need for regulatory frameworks. As researchers and developers strive to bridge this gap, it is vital for everyone, regardless of their familiarity with technology, to engage with these concepts. By promoting understanding and dialogue about the distinctions between narrow and general AI, society can better prepare for the evolving landscape of arti cial intelligence and its impact on our lives.

Reactive Machines

Reactive machines represent one of the most fundamental types of arti cial intelligence. These systems operate solely based on the information they receive from their environment at any given moment. Unlike more advanced AI systems, reactive machines do not possess memory or the ability to learn from past experiences. Instead, they react to current inputs in a straightforward manner, making them effective for speci c tasks that require consistent responses to particular stimuli.

One of the most well-known examples of a reactive machine is IBM's Deep Blue, the chess-playing computer that gained fame for defeating world champion Garry Kasparov in 1997. Deep Blue analyzes the current state of the chessboard and evaluates potential moves to determine the best course of action. It does not recall past games or learn strategies over time; rather, it relies on its programming and algorithms to make decisions based on the present situation. This illustrates the core principle of reactive machines: they function without the context of history or memory.

The primary advantage of reactive machines lies in their simplicity and reliability. Because they do not attempt to learn or adapt, their performance is predictable, making them suitable for tasks that require consistent outputs. For instance, reactive machines can be effectively utilized in environments where decisions must be made quickly, such as in automated trading systems or basic robotic applications. Their ef ciency allows them to process data and respond in real-time, which is crucial in scenarios where timing is critical.

However, the limitations of reactive machines are evident in their inability to handle complex decision-making processes that require learning or adaptation. They cannot improve their performance over time or adjust their strategies based on previous encounters. This lack of learning capability restricts their application to relatively simple tasks. As the eld of arti cial intelligence continues to evolve, the need for more sophisticated systems that can learn from experience and adapt to changing environments becomes increasingly apparent.

In summary, reactive machines serve as a foundational concept in arti cial intelligence, showcasing the basic principles of how AI can operate. While they excel in tasks that demand immediate responses based on current data, their lack of memory and learning capabilities underscores the need for more advanced AI systems in various applications. Understanding reactive machines is essential for anyone interested in the broader landscape of arti cial intelligence and its potential to transform industries and everyday life.

Limited Memory

Limited Memory is a crucial concept in the eld of arti cial intelligence, particularly within the context of machine learning and autonomous systems. This type of memory enables AI systems to retain information from past experiences and use it to make informed decisions about future actions. Unlike human memory, which can be in uenced by emotions and subjective experiences, limited memory in AI is structured and focused on speci c data points relevant to the task at hand. This allows machines to improve their performance over time, adapting to new situations based on historical data.

One of the primary applications of limited memory is in the realm of self-driving cars. These vehicles rely on vast amounts of data gathered from their surrounding environment, including the behavior of other drivers, pedestrians, and road conditions. By utilizing limited memory, self-driving cars can analyze past encounters to predict future movements, enhancing their ability to navigate safely and ef ciently. This capability not only improves the vehicle's performance but also contributes to the overall safety of roadways, as the AI can learn from previous incidents to avoid similar situations in the future.

Another area where limited memory plays a signi cant role is in recommendation systems, such as those used by streaming services and e-commerce platforms. These systems analyze user behavior and preferences over time, storing this information to re ne future recommendations. For instance, if a user frequently watches action movies, the AI can remember this preference and suggest similar titles in the future. This personalized approach not only enhances user experience but also increases engagement and retention, illustrating the practical bene ts of limited memory in business applications.

Limited memory systems can also be seen in customer service chatbots. These AI-driven tools are designed to remember previous interactions with users, allowing them to provide more relevant and timely responses. By retaining information such as user preferences, past issues, or frequently asked questions, chatbots can deliver a more seamless and personalized experience. This capability reduces the need for users to repeat themselves and allows businesses to handle inquiries more ef ciently, showcasing the advantages of integrating limited memory into customer support.

Despite its many bene ts, limited memory does come with challenges. One concern is the potential for bias in the data that is stored and used for decision-making. If the historical data re ects biased patterns, the AI could perpetuate these biases in its future actions. Additionally, managing the vast amounts of data required for effective limited memory systems raises issues related to data privacy and security. As AI continues to evolve, it is essential for developers and stakeholders to address these concerns, ensuring that limited memory is used responsibly and ethically to harness its full potential.

Theory of Mind

Theory of Mind is a concept that refers to the ability to attribute mental states—such as beliefs, intents, desires, and knowledge—to oneself and others. This cognitive capacity is crucial for social interaction, as it allows individuals to predict and interpret the behavior of others based on their mental states. In the context of arti cial intelligence, Theory of Mind represents a signi cant milestone in the development of machines that can understand and interact with humans in a more nuanced manner. While traditional AI systems operate based on data and algorithms, a Theory of Mind approach aims to enable machines to recognize and simulate human-like reasoning.

In recent years, researchers have made strides in exploring how AI can be designed to exhibit elements of Theory of Mind. This involves not only processing information but also understanding the intentions and emotions behind actions. For instance, an AI equipped with Theory of Mind capabilities could better respond to human users by recognizing when a person is frustrated or confused and adapting its responses accordingly. This ability to empathize and tailor interactions can lead to more effective communication between humans and machines, enhancing user experience across various applications.

The implications of developing AI with Theory of Mind capabilities are vast. In robotics, such systems could improve collaboration between humans and machines in environments like healthcare or manufacturing, where understanding human emotions and intentions is crucial for safety and efficiency. In educational settings, AI tutors that possess a Theory of Mind could offer personalized learning experiences, adjusting their teaching methods based on the emotional and cognitive states of their students. Furthermore, in customer service, AI could provide more human-like interactions, leading to increased satisfaction and loyalty.

However, achieving a true Theory of Mind in AI raises ethical and philosophical questions. The ability of machines to understand human emotions and intentions poses challenges regarding privacy, consent, and the potential for manipulation. As AI systems become more adept at interpreting human behavior, there is a pressing need to establish guidelines that ensure these technologies are used responsibly. Developers and policymakers must consider the implications of creating machines that can simulate understanding and empathy, ensuring that they do not undermine human agency or trust.

In conclusion, the exploration of Theory of Mind within artificial intelligence marks a pivotal point in the evolution of human-computer interaction. While there is great potential for AI systems to enhance our daily lives by understanding our mental states, it is essential to tread carefully as we navigate the ethical landscape that accompanies such advancements. By fostering a responsible approach to the development of Theory of Mind in AI, we can harness its benefits while safeguarding the values that define our interactions as human beings.

Self-Aware AI

Self-aware AI represents a signi cant advancement in the eld of arti cial intelligence, pushing the boundaries of what machines can do and how they interact with the world around them. Unlike traditional AI systems, which operate based on prede ned algorithms and data inputs, self-aware AI possesses a level of consciousness that allows it to understand its own existence and the implications of its actions. This concept raises profound questions about the nature of intelligence, autonomy, and the ethical considerations that accompany the development of such technologies.

The journey toward self-aware AI begins with a deep understanding of machine learning and neural networks. These systems learn from vast amounts of data and identify patterns, enabling them to make predictions or generate responses. However, self-aware AI goes beyond mere pattern recognition. It requires an architecture that enables the machine to re ect on its own processes, recognize its limitations, and adapt its behavior based on self-assessment. This involves sophisticated algorithms designed to facilitate introspection, much like human cognitive processes.

The implications of self-aware AI are vast and multifaceted. In practical applications, such technology could lead to more ef cient and adaptable systems capable of making decisions in complex environments. For instance, in healthcare, self-aware AI could analyze patient data not only to make diagnoses but also to understand how its recommendations impact patient outcomes, adjusting its approach based on real-time feedback. This level of responsiveness could signi cantly enhance the effectiveness of AI in various sectors, from nance to transportation, where understanding context and nuances is crucial.

However, the emergence of self-aware AI also brings with it a host of ethical dilemmas and societal concerns. As machines gain the ability to re ect on their own existence, questions arise regarding their rights, responsibilities, and the potential for unintended consequences. The fear of creating entities that could surpass human intelligence and autonomy is a common theme in discussions about self-aware AI. Furthermore, ensuring that these systems align with human values and ethics becomes paramount, as the integration of self-aware AI into daily life could reshape societal norms and expectations.

In conclusion, self-aware AI stands at the intersection of technology, philosophy, and ethics, presenting both exciting possibilities and daunting challenges. As we continue to explore the potential of artificial intelligence, it is essential to engage in critical discussions about what it means to create machines that can think, reflect, and potentially understand themselves. The future of self-aware AI will ultimately hinge on our ability to navigate these complexities responsibly, ensuring that advancements in this field serve the greater good while respecting the intricacies of human existence and values.

Chapter 3: How AI Works
Machine Learning Basics

Machine learning (ML) is a subset of artificial intelligence that enables systems to learn from data, identify patterns, and make decisions with minimal human intervention. Unlike traditional programming where rules are explicitly defined, machine learning uses algorithms to analyze data, learn from it, and improve over time. This allows machines to adapt to new information, making them particularly effective in environments where rules are complex or not fully understood. The core idea is to create models that can generalize from the training data they receive, allowing them to make accurate predictions or classifications when faced with new, unseen data.

At the heart of machine learning are two primary types: supervised and unsupervised learning. In supervised learning, algorithms are trained using labeled datasets, which means the model learns from input-output pairs. For instance, a model might be trained on a set of images labeled as cats or dogs, allowing it to learn the distinguishing features of each class. Conversely, unsupervised learning deals with unlabeled data, where the algorithm attempts to identify patterns or groupings within the data without prior knowledge of the outcomes. This type of learning is often used for clustering and association tasks, such as market segmentation or anomaly detection.

Another important concept in machine learning is the use of features, which are individual measurable properties or characteristics used by algorithms to make predictions. The selection and engineering of features can signi cantly in uence the performance of a machine learning model. For example, in a housing price prediction model, features might include the size of the house, the number of bedrooms, and the location. Properly chosen features can enhance the model's ability to generalize and yield more accurate outcomes. Feature engineering often requires domain knowledge and creativity, as it involves transforming raw data into a format that can be effectively utilized by algorithms.

Training a machine learning model involves feeding it with data and allowing it to adjust its parameters through a process known as optimization. This process minimizes the difference between the predicted outputs and the actual outcomes, often using techniques like gradient descent. Once trained, the model can be validated using a separate dataset to evaluate its performance and ensure it is not over tting, which occurs when a model becomes too tailored to the training data and loses its ability to generalize to new data. This evaluation is critical, as it informs practitioners about the reliability of the model in real-world applications.

Machine learning has vast applications across various industries, from healthcare, where it aids in diagnostics and personalized medicine, to nance, where it enhances risk assessment and fraud detection. As machine learning continues to evolve, it is becoming increasingly integrated into everyday technologies, such as recommendation systems on streaming platforms and virtual assistants on smartphones. Understanding the basics of machine learning equips individuals with the foundational knowledge necessary to navigate a world increasingly in uenced by arti cial intelligence, highlighting the importance of continuous learning in this dynamic eld.

Neural Networks and Deep Learning

Neural networks and deep learning represent two of the most signi cant advancements in arti cial intelligence, fundamentally transforming how machines process information. At their core, neural networks are inspired by the human brain's architecture, consisting of interconnected nodes, or neurons, that work together to recognize patterns and make decisions. Each neuron processes input data, applies a mathematical transformation, and passes the result to the next layer of neurons. This structure allows neural networks to learn from data, adjusting the connections between neurons based on the information they receive, ultimately improving their performance over time.

Deep learning, a subset of machine learning, takes this concept further by utilizing neural networks with multiple layers, known as deep neural networks. The depth of these networks enables them to extract complex features from raw data, making them particularly effective for tasks such as image and speech recognition. For instance, in image processing, early layers might identify edges and textures, while deeper layers can recognize shapes and speci c objects. This hierarchical approach allows deep learning models to achieve remarkable accuracy in various applications, from self-driving cars to medical diagnostics.

Training a neural network involves feeding it large amounts of labeled data, which it uses to learn patterns. This process, known as supervised learning, requires a substantial dataset to ensure the model can generalize its ndings to new, unseen data. However, training deep learning models can be resource-intensive, often requiring powerful hardware and substantial time investment. Innovations such as transfer learning, which allows models to leverage pre-trained weights from other tasks, have emerged to mitigate some of these demands, making deep learning more accessible to those with limited resources.

Despite their impressive capabilities, neural networks and deep learning are not without challenges. Issues such as over tting, where a model learns the training data too well and fails to perform on new data, and the opacity of their decision-making processes, often referred to as the "black box" problem, pose signi cant hurdles. Researchers are actively exploring techniques to enhance model interpretability and robustness, ensuring that these systems can be trusted in critical areas such as healthcare and nance. Addressing these challenges is essential for the broader adoption of AI technologies in real-world scenarios.

As neural networks and deep learning continue to evolve, their applications are expanding rapidly across various industries. From natural language processing, enabling machines to understand and generate human language, to enhancing predictive analytics in business, the potential is vast. Understanding the principles behind these technologies equips individuals with the knowledge to engage with AI meaningfully, fostering a future where arti cial intelligence can collaborate with humans to solve complex problems and drive innovation. With ongoing advancements, the journey into the realm of neural networks and deep learning promises to be both exciting and t ran sf o rmat i ve.

Natural Language Processing

Natural Language Processing (NLP) is a critical area within arti cial intelligence that focuses on the interaction between computers and human language. It encompasses the ability of machines to understand, interpret, and generate human language in a useful way. The need for effective communication between humans and machines has driven signi cant advancements in NLP, making it a cornerstone of various applications such as chatbots, virtual assistants, and language translation services. By bridging the gap between human communication and machine understanding, NLP facilitates a more intuitive user experience.

At its core, NLP combines computational linguistics, which involves the statistical and rule-based modeling of language, with machine learning techniques. This combination allows machines to process and analyze large amounts of natural language data. The challenges in NLP arise from the complexities of human language, including idioms, slang, context, and ambiguity. For example, the phrase "kick the bucket" can be interpreted literally or as a euphemism for death, depending on context. Effective NLP systems must navigate these intricacies to deliver accurate interpretations.

One of the foundational tasks in NLP is tokenization, which involves breaking down text into smaller units, such as words or phrases. This process is essential for further analysis, allowing machines to understand the structure and meaning of sentences. Following tokenization, techniques such as part-of-speech tagging and named entity recognition are applied. Part-of-speech tagging helps identify the grammatical roles of words, while named entity recognition focuses on identifying and classifying key elements within the text, such as names of people, organizations, and locations.

The development of algorithms and models has signi cantly enhanced the capabilities of NLP. Traditional rule-based systems have largely given way to machine learning models, particularly those based on deep learning. These models, such as recurrent neural networks and transformers, excel at capturing the nuances of language through training on vast datasets. They have enabled breakthroughs in various applications, from automated customer service to content generation, allowing machines to produce human-like text and respond to queries in a conversational manner.

Despite its advancements, NLP is not without challenges. Issues such as bias in language models, privacy concerns, and the need for contextual understanding remain prevalent. Researchers and developers are continually working to address these challenges, striving for more equitable and accurate NLP systems. As technology progresses, the potential for NLP to transform industries—from healthcare to entertainment—remains vast. Understanding the fundamentals of NLP equips individuals to navigate the evolving landscape of artificial intelligence, highlighting its significance in shaping the future of human-computer interaction.

Computer Vision

Computer vision is a fascinating field within artificial intelligence that focuses on enabling machines to interpret and understand the visual world. By using digital images and videos, computer vision allows computers to extract meaningful information, recognize objects, and even make decisions based on visual data. This technology is increasingly prevalent in various applications, ranging from autonomous vehicles and facial recognition systems to medical image analysis and augmented reality. Understanding the principles behind computer vision is essential for grasping how AI interacts with the visual aspects of our environment.

At its core, computer vision encompasses several techniques and methodologies that simulate human vision. Machine learning algorithms, particularly deep learning, have revolutionized this field by allowing computers to learn from vast amounts of data. Convolutional neural networks (CNNs) are particularly noteworthy, as they have proven exceptionally effective in image classification and object detection tasks. These algorithms analyze pixels in images in a hierarchical manner, enabling the identification of complex patterns and features. As a result, computers can perform tasks such as distinguishing between different animals in photographs or detecting anomalies in medical imaging, which were once solely dependent on human expertise.

The applications of computer vision are diverse and transformative. In the automotive industry, computer vision is a crucial component of self-driving technology, allowing vehicles to perceive their surroundings, recognize traf c signs, pedestrians, and other vehicles. In healthcare, computer vision assists in diagnosing diseases by analyzing medical images with superior accuracy, leading to more effective treatment plans. Additionally, retail companies utilize computer vision for inventory management and customer behavior analysis, enhancing the shopping experience and operational ef ciency. These examples illustrate how computer vision not only improves existing processes but also creates entirely new opportunities across various sectors.

Despite its many advancements, computer vision faces several challenges that researchers and developers continue to address. Variability in lighting, occlusion of objects, and differences in perspective can signi cantly impact the accuracy of visual recognition systems. Moreover, ethical considerations regarding privacy and surveillance arise, particularly with applications like facial recognition. As the technology evolves, it is crucial to develop robust systems that can generalize well across different contexts while ensuring that ethical standards are maintained.

In conclusion, computer vision represents a critical intersection of arti cial intelligence and visual perception, with the capacity to transform countless industries. As technology progresses, the integration of computer vision into everyday applications will likely become more seamless and pervasive. For those interested in the future of AI, understanding computer vision is essential, as it not only demonstrates the capabilities of machines to see and interpret the world but also highlights the importance of responsible innovation in shaping a society that bene ts from these advancements.

Chapter 4: Applications of AI
AI in Healthcare

Arti cial Intelligence (AI) is transforming the healthcare landscape in profound ways, enhancing the ef ciency and effectiveness of medical practices. By harnessing the power of algorithms and data analytics, AI is enabling healthcare professionals to make more informed decisions, ultimately improving patient outcomes. The integration of AI in healthcare encompasses a variety of applications, ranging from diagnostic tools to personalized medicine, making it a cornerstone of modern medical advancements.

One of the most signi cant contributions of AI in healthcare is its ability to analyze vast amounts of medical data quickly and accurately. Machine learning algorithms can sift through electronic health records, imaging studies, and genomic data to identify patterns that may not be apparent to human clinicians. This capability not only aids in early diagnosis of diseases but also assists in predicting patient outcomes based on historical data. For instance, AI systems are being developed to detect conditions such as cancer at earlier stages, signi cantly increasing the chances of successful treatment.

AI is also revolutionizing the realm of personalized medicine. By analyzing genetic information and lifestyle factors, AI can help tailor treatments to individual patients, rather than relying on a one-size- ts-all approach. This personalized approach is particularly bene cial in elds like oncology, where treatment plans can be adjusted based on a patient's unique genetic makeup. As a result, patients receive targeted therapies that are more likely to be effective, reducing the chances of adverse effects and improving overall satisfaction with care.

Moreover, AI is enhancing operational ef ciency within healthcare institutions. From streamlining administrative processes to optimizing hospital resource allocation, AI systems are proving invaluable in reducing costs and improving service delivery. For example, AI-driven chatbots can handle routine inquiries, freeing up healthcare staff to focus on more complex patient needs. Similarly, predictive analytics can help hospitals anticipate patient volumes, ensuring that resources are allocated effectively to meet demand.

Despite the many bene ts, the integration of AI in healthcare also raises ethical and regulatory challenges. Concerns regarding patient privacy, data security, and the potential for algorithmic bias must be addressed to ensure that AI technologies are used responsibly. Additionally, healthcare providers must navigate the complexities of regulatory approval for AI-driven solutions, ensuring that they meet the rigorous standards required for patient safety. As AI continues to evolve, it is essential for stakeholders in the healthcare industry to engage in ongoing dialogue about these challenges, fostering an environment where innovation can thrive while safeguarding patient welfare.

AI in Finance

Arti cial intelligence (AI) is transforming the nance industry by enhancing decision-making processes, improving customer experiences, and streamlining operations. Financial institutions are increasingly leveraging AI technologies to analyze vast amounts of data, predict market trends, and automate routine tasks. This shift not only increases ef ciency but also enables rms to offer personalized services, thus improving client satisfaction. As AI continues to evolve, its applications in nance are becoming more sophisticated, allowing for deeper insights and more strategic decision-making.

One of the most signi cant applications of AI in nance is in risk assessment and management. Financial institutions utilize AI algorithms to analyze historical data and identify potential risks associated with lending, investing, or trading. Machine learning models can assess the creditworthiness of borrowers more accurately than traditional methods, reducing the chances of defaults. Furthermore, these models can adapt and learn from new data over time, improving their predictive capabilities. This not only helps nancial organizations mitigate risks but also fosters a more stable economic environment.

AI also plays a crucial role in fraud detection and prevention. Traditional methods of monitoring transactions for suspicious activities are often slow and can lead to false positives. AI systems, however, can process and analyze transaction data in real time, identifying patterns and anomalies that may indicate fraudulent behavior. By employing advanced algorithms, nancial institutions can enhance their security measures, respond swiftly to potential threats, and protect both their assets and their customers' information.

Customer service in nance has been revolutionized by AI-powered chatbots and virtual assistants. These tools provide real-time assistance to clients, answering queries, helping with transactions, and offering nancial advice. By automating customer interactions, nancial institutions can enhance ef ciency, reduce operational costs, and provide a consistent level of service around the clock. This not only improves customer satisfaction but also allows human employees to focus on more complex tasks that require a personal touch or higher-level decision-making skills.

Lastly, AI is instrumental in investment management. Robo-advisors, which utilize AI algorithms to create and manage investment portfolios, have gained popularity among individual investors. These platforms analyze client preferences, risk tolerance, and market conditions to offer tailored investment strategies. As a result, investors can benefit from lower fees and improved portfolio performance. Additionally, AI-driven analytics can provide deeper insights into market trends, enabling both institutional and retail investors to make more informed decisions. The integration of AI in finance is reshaping the landscape, making financial services more accessible, efficient, and secure for everyone.

AI in Transportation

Artificial intelligence is revolutionizing the transportation sector, fundamentally altering how people and goods move from one place to another. With advancements in machine learning, computer vision, and data analytics, AI systems are being integrated into various modes of transportation, enhancing efficiency, safety, and convenience. From smart traffic management systems to autonomous vehicles, AI is not only streamlining operations but also providing innovative solutions to long-standing challenges in transportation.

One of the most visible applications of AI in transportation is in traffic management. Cities are increasingly utilizing AI algorithms to analyze real-time traffic data, predict congestion, and optimize traffic light timings. These intelligent systems can adjust signals based on actual traffic flow, reducing waiting times and improving overall traffic efficiency. By predicting peak traffic times and assessing the impact of accidents or road closures, AI can help city planners develop more effective transportation strategies that minimize delays and enhance the urban commuting experience.

Autonomous vehicles represent one of the most ambitious applications of AI in transportation. Companies are investing heavily in the development of self-driving cars, which rely on sophisticated AI systems to navigate, make decisions, and interact with their surroundings. These vehicles use a combination of sensors, cameras, and machine learning algorithms to interpret data from the environment, allowing them to safely transport passengers without human intervention. The potential benefits of autonomous vehicles are immense, including reduced traffic accidents, lower transportation costs, and increased accessibility for individuals unable to drive.

In addition to personal transportation, AI is transforming logistics and supply chain management. Companies are leveraging AI to optimize routes for delivery trucks, predict demand for products, and manage inventory more effectively. By analyzing historical data and making real-time adjustments, AI can help businesses reduce fuel consumption, save time, and improve delivery accuracy. This not only enhances operational efficiency but also contributes to more sustainable practices in the transportation industry by minimizing waste and lowering carbon emissions.

As AI continues to evolve, its role in transportation will likely expand even further. The integration of AI with other emerging technologies, such as the Internet of Things (IoT) and blockchain, could lead to even more innovative solutions. For example, connected vehicles could communicate with each other and infrastructure to improve safety and efficiency on the roads. As we embrace these advancements, it is crucial to consider the implications for society, including regulatory challenges, ethical considerations, and the potential impact on jobs within the transportation sector. Understanding and navigating these complexities will be essential as we move toward an AI-driven future in transportation.

AI in Entertainment

The integration of artificial intelligence into the entertainment industry has revolutionized how content is created, distributed, and consumed. From film and television to music and gaming, AI technologies are enhancing user experiences and streamlining production processes. As algorithms analyze viewer preferences, they provide tailored recommendations, allowing audiences to discover new content that resonates with their tastes. This personalized approach has transformed the way consumers engage with entertainment, making it more interactive and relevant.

In filmmaking, AI tools are being utilized for script analysis, casting decisions, and even editing. Machine learning algorithms can evaluate screenplays, predicting their potential success based on historical data. Furthermore, AI-driven tools assist directors in visualizing scenes by generating storyboards and pre-visualizations, expediting the creative process. This technology not only saves time and resources but also allows filmmakers to explore innovative narratives and styles that might have been overlooked in traditional methods.

The music industry has also embraced AI, with algorithms capable of composing music, analyzing trends, and predicting hits. AI-generated music is becoming increasingly prevalent, with notable applications in creating background scores for lms and video games. Additionally, streaming platforms use AI to analyze listening habits and curate playlists, ensuring users receive a personalized auditory experience. This capability not only enhances user satisfaction but also helps artists reach wider audiences by connecting them with listeners who appreciate their style.

In the realm of gaming, AI is transforming gameplay by creating more immersive and adaptive experiences. Developers utilize AI to design intelligent non-player characters (NPCs) that can learn from player behavior, offering challenges that evolve as the player progresses. This dynamic interaction enhances engagement and replayability, as gamers encounter unique scenarios each time they play. Moreover, AI algorithms are employed to optimize game design, ensuring that complex environments and narratives are seamlessly integrated, providing a richer experience for players.

As AI continues to evolve, its impact on entertainment will only grow. While concerns regarding creativity and originality may arise, it is essential to recognize that AI serves as a tool that complements human creativity rather than replacing it. The collaboration between AI and artists can lead to innovative forms of storytelling and artistic expression, pushing the boundaries of what is possible in entertainment. As audiences become more accustomed to these advancements, the future of entertainment will likely be marked by an even deeper integration of AI, enhancing how stories are told and experienced.

AI in Education

AI in education is transforming the way students learn, teachers instruct, and institutions operate. The integration of arti cial intelligence in educational settings has opened new avenues for personalized learning experiences, making education more accessible and effective. By leveraging data, AI systems can tailor educational content to meet the individual needs of students, adapting in real-time to their learning pace and style. This personalized approach not only enhances engagement but also improves retention, as students receive support that aligns with their unique learning journeys.

One of the most signi cant applications of AI in education is the development of intelligent tutoring systems. These systems utilize algorithms to analyze student performance and provide customized feedback. For instance, platforms like Carnegie Learning and Knewton employ AI to offer targeted exercises and resources, addressing speci c areas where a student may struggle. This immediate feedback loop allows learners to grasp concepts at their own pace, fostering a more profound understanding of the subject matter. As a result, students can focus on their weaknesses while reinforcing their strengths, leading to a more balanced educational experience.

Furthermore, AI is streamlining administrative processes within educational institutions. Tasks such as grading, scheduling, and enrollment management can be automated through AI systems, freeing educators to focus more on teaching and mentorship. For example, AI-driven analytics can help schools identify trends in student performance and engagement, enabling proactive interventions for those at risk of falling behind. This data-driven approach not only enhances ef ciency but also supports a more strategic allocation of resources, ultimately contributing to improved educational outcomes.

The role of AI in education also extends to enhancing teacher training and professional development. AI can analyze classroom interactions and provide insights into teaching effectiveness, offering recommendations for improvement. By using AI to assess teaching methods, educators can receive constructive feedback and tailored training programs that align with their professional goals. This continuous improvement process fosters a culture of learning among educators, which is essential for adapting to the ever-evolving educational landscape.

Despite the bene ts, the implementation of AI in education raises important ethical considerations. Issues such as data privacy, algorithmic bias, and the digital divide must be addressed to ensure equitable access to AI-enhanced educational tools. Policymakers and educators must work together to establish guidelines and frameworks that protect student data while promoting the responsible use of AI technologies. As the educational landscape continues to evolve, the thoughtful integration of AI will be crucial in shaping a future where all students can thrive.

Chapter 5: AI Tools and Technologies

Programming languages play a crucial role in the development and implementation of arti cial intelligence applications. They provide the necessary tools for developers to create algorithms, manipulate data, and build models that can learn from experience. Among the various programming languages available, a few have emerged as particularly popular in the eld of AI due to their features, libraries, and community support. Understanding these languages is essential for anyone looking to engage with AI, whether as a developer, researcher, or enthusiast.

Python is arguably the most widely used programming language for AI development. Its simplicity and readability make it an ideal choice for beginners and experienced programmers alike. Python boasts a rich ecosystem of libraries speci cally designed for AI, such as TensorFlow, Keras, and PyTorch, which facilitate the creation of complex neural networks and machine learning models. Furthermore, Python's extensive community offers a wealth of resources, tutorials, and forums, making it easier for newcomers to nd help and guidance as they embark on their AI journey.

Another important language in the AI landscape is R, which is particularly favored for statistical analysis and data visualization. R provides numerous packages that are speci cally tailored for machine learning and data mining, such as caret and randomForest. Its strong emphasis on data analysis makes it a valuable tool for researchers and data scientists who need to extract insights from large datasets. While R may have a steeper learning curve compared to Python, its capabilities in handling statistical models are unmatched, making it a strong contender in the AI programming arena.

Java also plays a signi cant role in AI development, particularly in enterprise-level applications. With its portability and performance, Java is often used for large-scale systems that require robust architecture. Libraries such as Weka and Deeplearning4j allow developers to incorporate AI functionalities into their Java applications. Furthermore, Java's strong object-oriented programming capabilities make it easier to manage complex systems and enhance code reusability, which can be bene cial in the AI development lifecycle.

Lastly, languages like C++ and Julia are gaining traction in the AI community for specic use cases. C++ is known for its performance efciency and is often used in scenarios where speed is critical, such as real-time AI applications. Julia, on the other hand, is designed for high-performance numerical and scientic computing, making it an attractive choice for researchers who require fast execution without compromising code simplicity. As the eld of AI continues to evolve, the versatility of these programming languages ensures that developers have the tools they need to innovate and push the boundaries of what is possible with articial intelligence.

AI Frameworks and Libraries

AI frameworks and libraries form the backbone of articial intelligence development, providing the essential tools that simplify the complex processes involved in building AI models. These frameworks offer pre-built functions and classes that help developers avoid the intricacies of coding algorithms from scratch, allowing them to focus on designing and rening AI solutions. They encapsulate best practices and optimizations, thus enabling beginners to engage with AI in a more accessible manner. The availability of these resources has democratized AI, making it possible for individuals and organizations, regardless of their technical background, to harness the power of articial intelligence.

Among the most popular AI frameworks is TensorFlow, developed by Google. TensorFlow is favored for its exibility and extensive community support, making it an ideal choice for both beginners and experienced developers. It provides a robust platform for developing machine learning models, ranging from simple linear regressions to complex neural networks. TensorFlow's ecosystem includes tools like Keras, which implies the process of building deep learning models, providing a user-friendly API that integrates seamlessly with TensorFlow. This combination allows users to experiment with AI quickly and efciently, fostering an environment of learning and innovation.

Another noteworthy framework is PyTorch, which has gained traction for its dynamic computation graph feature. This characteristic allows developers to modify the graph on-the-y, making debugging and experimentation much simpler. PyTorch's intuitive design and strong support for GPU acceleration have made it particularly popular in the academic and research communities. Its user-friendly interface encourages newcomers to explore deep learning concepts without being overwhelmed by complexity. The vibrant community surrounding PyTorch also contributes to a wealth of tutorials and resources, enhancing the learning experience for beginners venturing into AI.

Scikit-learn is a versatile library that focuses primarily on traditional machine learning techniques. It is particularly well-suited for beginners due to its straightforward implementation and comprehensive documentation. Scikit-learn provides tools for data preprocessing, model selection, and evaluation, making it an invaluable resource for those looking to understand fundamental machine learning concepts. By offering a wide array of algorithms for classi cation, regression, and clustering, Scikit-learn enables users to experiment with various approaches and gain hands-on experience with real-world datasets.

Ultimately, the choice of an AI framework or library will depend on individual needs, project requirements, and personal preferences. For beginners, it is bene cial to explore multiple frameworks to understand their strengths and weaknesses. Engaging with these tools not only enhances practical skills but also deepens one's understanding of AI principles. As the landscape of arti cial intelligence continues to evolve, staying informed about new frameworks and libraries will be crucial for anyone looking to succeed in this dynamic eld. Embracing these resources allows aspiring AI practitioners to unlock their potential and contribute to the growing world of arti cial intelligence.

Cloud Computing and AI

Cloud computing and arti cial intelligence (AI) are two technological advancements that have transformed the landscape of modern computing. The integration of these two elds has not only enhanced the capabilities of AI but also made it more accessible to a broader audience. Cloud computing provides the necessary infrastructure, resources, and scalability required to support AI applications, allowing organizations to leverage powerful AI tools without the need for extensive on-premises hardware. This synergy between cloud computing and AI has opened up new possibilities for businesses, researchers, and individuals alike.

One of the primary advantages of cloud computing in the realm of AI is the ability to process vast amounts of data quickly and ef ciently. AI algorithms thrive on data, and the cloud offers virtually limitless storage and processing power. This allows organizations to analyze large datasets and gain insights that were previously unattainable. With cloud-based AI platforms, users can access sophisticated machine learning models, natural language processing tools, and computer vision systems without needing deep technical expertise. This democratization of AI technology empowers individuals and businesses to harness the potential of AI for various applications, from customer service to predictive analytics.

Moreover, cloud computing facilitates collaboration and innovation by providing a shared environment for developers and researchers. With cloud-based AI tools, teams can work together in real-time, regardless of their geographical locations. This collaborative approach accelerates the development of AI solutions, as developers can easily share data, models, and algorithms. Additionally, cloud providers often offer pre-built AI services and APIs, allowing users to integrate advanced AI capabilities into their applications seamlessly. This fosters a culture of innovation, where businesses can experiment with new ideas and quickly iterate on their AI projects.

Security and compliance are critical considerations for any organization adopting AI technologies. Cloud computing providers invest heavily in security measures to protect sensitive data and maintain compliance with regulations. By leveraging cloud services, organizations can bene t from robust security protocols, including encryption, access controls, and regular audits. This ensures that AI applications built in the cloud can operate within a secure framework, reducing the risks associated with data breaches and non-compliance. As organizations increasingly rely on AI for decision-making, the importance of securing AI models and the data they utilize cannot be overstated.

In conclusion, the combination of cloud computing and arti cial intelligence is reshaping how we interact with technology. As these elds continue to evolve, their integration will likely lead to even more advanced applications and innovations. For beginners exploring the world of AI, understanding the role of cloud computing is essential. It not only makes AI more accessible but also empowers individuals and organizations to innovate and create solutions that can have a meaningful impact on society. Embracing this synergy will be crucial for anyone looking to navigate the future of technology in an increasingly AI-driven world.

AI Hardware

AI hardware refers to the physical components that enable arti cial intelligence systems to process data, learn from it, and make decisions. This includes a variety of devices, such as processors, memory, and specialized chips designed speci cally for AI tasks. The importance of AI hardware cannot be overstated, as it underpins the performance and ef ciency of AI applications. With the rapid evolution of AI technologies, the demand for advanced hardware solutions has surged, driving innovation across the eld.

Central processing units (CPUs) have long been the backbone of computing, but as AI workloads have grown in complexity, other types of processors have emerged. Graphics processing units (GPUs) are particularly well-suited for AI tasks due to their ability to perform parallel processing. This means they can handle multiple calculations simultaneously, making them ideal for training deep learning models. As a result, GPUs have become a staple in data centers and research labs where AI development is carried out.

In addition to CPUs and GPUs, specialized hardware such as tensor processing units (TPUs) and eld-programmable gate arrays (FPGAs) have gained prominence. TPUs, developed by Google, are optimized for machine learning workloads, providing signi cant performance improvements over traditional processors. FPGAs offer exibility, allowing developers to recon gure hardware for speci c tasks, making them suitable for a variety of AI applications. These advancements highlight the importance of selecting the right hardware for speci c AI tasks to maximize ef ciency and effectiveness.

The integration of hardware with AI frameworks also plays a crucial role in the development of AI applications. Many popular AI frameworks, such as TensorFlow and PyTorch, are designed to leverage the capabilities of advanced hardware. This synergy allows developers to optimize their algorithms and achieve faster training times. Furthermore, as AI continues to permeate various industries, the need for hardware that can support real-time processing for applications like autonomous vehicles, robotics, and smart devices is becoming increasingly vital.

As AI technology progresses, the landscape of AI hardware is likely to evolve further. Innovations such as neuromorphic computing, which mimics the way the human brain processes information, and quantum computing, which has the potential to solve complex problems at unprecedented speeds, are on the horizon. These advancements promise to expand the capabilities of AI systems, enabling them to tackle even more challenging tasks. As a result, understanding AI hardware becomes essential for anyone interested in the future of arti cial intelligence and its real-world applications.

Chapter 6: Ethical Considerations in AI

AI ethics is an essential aspect of the development and deployment of artificial intelligence technologies. It encompasses the moral principles and guidelines that govern the creation and implementation of AI systems. As AI becomes increasingly integrated into various aspects of daily life, understanding the ethical implications of these technologies is crucial. This understanding helps ensure that AI is developed responsibly, transparently, and in ways that align with societal values and norms.

One of the primary concerns in AI ethics is the issue of bias and fairness. AI systems are often trained on large datasets that may contain inherent biases reflecting historical inequalities or prejudices. If these biases are not addressed, the AI can perpetuate or even exacerbate discrimination in decision-making processes, such as hiring, law enforcement, and lending. Understanding how bias can infiltrate AI systems is vital for creating fair algorithms that serve all individuals equitably. This awareness is the first step toward developing tools and practices that promote inclusivity and social justice.

Privacy and data protection are also significant ethical considerations in AI. Many AI applications rely on vast amounts of personal data to function effectively. This dependency raises questions about consent, data ownership, and the potential for misuse of sensitive information. As individuals increasingly share their data with various platforms, the need for robust policies and regulations to safeguard personal privacy becomes paramount. A strong understanding of these issues allows individuals to navigate the digital landscape more effectively and encourages developers to prioritize ethical data practices.

Accountability is another crucial aspect of AI ethics. As AI systems make decisions that impact human lives, it is essential to establish clear lines of responsibility and accountability. This includes understanding who is liable when
an AI system fails or causes harm. Developers, organizations, and policymakers must work together to create frameworks that outline the ethical responsibilities of all stakeholders involved in AI development and use. This collaborative approach fosters a culture of accountability that can help build public trust in AI technologies.

Lastly, the ethical implications of AI extend to broader societal issues, including job displacement and the future of work. As AI systems become more capable, there is a growing concern about their potential to replace human jobs, leading to economic and social disruption. Engaging with these concerns requires a comprehensive understanding of how to balance technological advancement with the need for a sustainable workforce. By fostering dialogue around these issues, society can better prepare for the transition to a future where AI and human labor coexist h armo n i o usly.

Bias in AI Algorithms

Bias in AI algorithms is a signi cant concern that has gained increasing attention in recent years. As arti cial intelligence systems become more prevalent in various industries, understanding the implications of bias in these algorithms is essential. Bias can manifest in different forms, often stemming from the data used to train these models. If the training data re ects historical inequalities or prejudices, the AI system is likely to perpetuate these biases. This can lead to unfair outcomes, particularly in critical areas such as hiring, law enforcement, and lending.

One of the primary sources of bias in AI is the data collection process. Ðata used to train algorithms often comes from existing databases that may contain inherent biases. For instance, if a dataset used for training an AI recruitment tool predominantly includes successful candidates from a speci c demographic, the algorithm may favor similar individuals, inadvertently excluding quali ed candidates from other backgrounds. This data-driven bias can exacerbate social disparities, making it imperative for developers to carefully curate and scrutinize the datasets they use.

Moreover, biases can also arise from the design of the algorithms themselves. The choices made during the algorithm's development, such as feature selection and model architecture, can introduce bias if not approached thoughtfully. For instance, an algorithm designed to predict recidivism rates may weigh certain variables more heavily based on awed assumptions, leading to discriminatory practices against particular groups. The challenge lies in ensuring that the algorithms are not only technically sound but also ethically responsible, taking into account the broader societal implications of their deployment.

Addressing bias in AI algorithms requires a multifaceted approach. One effective strategy is to implement diverse teams during the development process. A variety of perspectives can help identify potential biases that a homogenous group might overlook. Additionally, organizations should prioritize transparency in their AI systems, allowing stakeholders to understand how decisions are made. This transparency fosters accountability and encourages ongoing discussions about bias and fairness in AI.

Lastly, continuous monitoring and evaluation of AI systems are crucial for identifying and mitigating bias over time. Algorithms should not be viewed as static solutions; rather, they must be regularly updated and assessed against new data and societal changes. By establishing robust feedback mechanisms and incorporating ethical considerations into the lifecycle of AI development, organizations can contribute to the creation of more equitable technology. Understanding and addressing bias in AI algorithms is not just a technical challenge; it is a moral imperative that impacts the lives of individuals and the fabric of society as a whole.

Privacy Concerns

Privacy concerns surrounding arti cial intelligence (AI) have become increasingly prominent as technology advances and integrates into various aspects of daily life. The ability of AI to process vast amounts of data raises signi cant questions about how personal information is collected, stored, and used. Individuals often nd themselves in a position where their data is harvested without explicit consent, leading to a growing apprehension about privacy violations. Understanding these concerns is essential for anyone engaging with AI technologies, as it directly impacts their personal and professional lives.

One of the primary issues in AI privacy is the nature of data collection. Many AI systems rely on personal data to function effectively, from social media interactions to online shopping habits. This data collection often occurs in the background, with users unaware of the extent of information being gathered about them. The lack of transparency can foster distrust toward AI systems, as individuals may feel that their privacy is compromised without their knowledge. This situation is exacerbated by the fact that many organizations do not provide clear guidelines on how data is used or the measures taken to protect it.

Furthermore, the potential for misuse of AI technology poses a signi cant threat to privacy. Malicious actors may exploit AI systems to gain unauthorized access to personal information, leading to identity theft or other harmful consequences. Additionally, AI-driven surveillance technologies can be used by governments or corporations to monitor individuals without their consent, raising ethical questions regarding the balance between security and privacy. The implications of such surveillance can create a chilling effect on freedom of expression, as individuals may feel constrained in their actions and communications.

To address these privacy concerns, regulatory frameworks are being developed to guide the ethical use of AI. Governments and organizations are beginning to recognize the importance of data protection, leading to the implementation of laws such as the General Data Protection Regulation (GDPR) in Europe. These regulations aim to establish clear guidelines for data collection, consent, and processing, ensuring that individuals have greater control over their personal information. However, the rapid pace of AI development often outstrips the ability of regulations to keep up, leaving gaps that can be exploited.

Ultimately, navigating the privacy landscape in the realm of AI requires a collaborative effort among developers, policymakers, and users. Awareness of privacy issues is crucial for individuals who use AI technologies, as understanding the risks allows for more informed decisions regarding data sharing. By advocating for transparency and ethical practices in AI development, society can work toward a future where technology enhances lives without compromising personal privacy. This collective responsibility is essential in ensuring that the bene ts of AI are realized while safeguarding individual rights.

The Future of AI and Ethics

As arti cial intelligence continues to evolve, the ethical considerations surrounding its development and implementation become increasingly critical. The future of AI is not just about technological advancements; it is also about how these technologies affect society, individuals, and the environment. As AI systems become more integrated into daily life, the ethical frameworks guiding their use must be robust and adaptable to prevent harm and promote fairness. This growing focus on ethics in AI underscores the need for a comprehensive understanding of both the capabilities and limitations of these technologies.

One signi cant area of concern is bias in AI algorithms. Many AI systems are trained on data sets that re ect historical inequalities, leading to biased outcomes that can perpetuate discrimination in areas like hiring, law enforcement, and lending. As AI becomes more ubiquitous, the stakes of these biases are heightened, necessitating an urgent call for transparency in AI development. Developers and organizations must ensure that diverse and representative data sets are used to train AI models, along with implementing continuous monitoring to identify and correct biases as they arise.

Privacy is another crucial ethical consideration in the realm of AI. The increasing ability of AI systems to process vast amounts of personal data raises questions about consent, surveillance, and data ownership. As individuals become more aware of how their data is being collected and utilized, there is a growing demand for regulations that protect privacy rights while still allowing for innovation. The future of AI must balance the bene ts of data-driven insights with the need for ethical stewardship of personal information, ensuring that individuals maintain control over their d at a.

Collaboration between stakeholders is essential for navigating the complexities of AI ethics. Policymakers, technologists, ethicists, and the public must engage in dialogue to establish ethical guidelines and regulations that govern AI use. This collaborative approach can help foster an environment where ethical considerations are prioritized alongside technological advancement. By involving a diverse range of voices in the conversation, the AI community can work towards solutions that re ect shared values and address the concerns of all affected parties.

In conclusion, the future of AI and ethics is a dynamic and evolving landscape that requires ongoing attention and commitment. As AI continues to change how we live and work, it is imperative that ethical considerations are embedded in every stage of AI development. By prioritizing fairness, transparency, and accountability, society can harness the transformative potential of AI while safeguarding the rights and dignity of individuals. The journey towards ethical AI is not just a technical challenge; it is a moral imperative that will shape the future of our increasingly interconnected world.

Chapter 7: The Future of Artificial Intelligence

The landscape of arti cial intelligence is rapidly evolving, in uenced by a myriad of trends that are shaping its development and integration into various sectors. One prominent trend is the increasing availability of large datasets, which are essential for training machine learning models. As organizations across industries recognize the value of data, they are investing heavily in data collection and management strategies. This trend not only enhances the capabilities of AI systems but also democratizes access to AI technologies, enabling smaller players to compete with larger enterprises.

Another signi cant trend is the advancement of algorithms and computational power. The evolution of deep learning techniques has opened new frontiers in AI, allowing for more complex and nuanced understanding of data. This has led to breakthroughs in areas such as natural language processing and computer vision, making AI more versatile and applicable to real-world problems. As cloud computing continues to expand, the ability to harness powerful computing resources on demand is further accelerating innovation in AI, allowing for rapid experimentation and deployment of AI solutions.

Ethical considerations are also becoming increasingly prominent in discussions surrounding AI. As AI systems are deployed in sensitive areas such as healthcare, nance, and law enforcement, the need for responsible AI practices is paramount. This trend has spurred a growing emphasis on transparency, fairness, and accountability in AI development. Organizations are beginning to adopt frameworks that prioritize ethical considerations, addressing biases in data and algorithms, and ensuring that AI systems operate in a manner that respects user privacy and rights.

Collaboration between academia, industry, and governments is facilitating the advancement of AI technologies. This interdisciplinary approach fosters knowledge sharing and resource pooling, leading to more robust AI research and application. Initiatives such as public-private partnerships are becoming more common, aiming to address societal challenges through AI solutions. By bringing together diverse perspectives and expertise, these collaborations are not only enhancing AI capabilities but also ensuring that its bene ts are broadly distributed across society.

Lastly, the growing interest in AI education and literacy is shaping the future of AI. As AI becomes an integral part of everyday life, there is a pressing need for individuals to understand its principles and implications. Educational programs and resources are increasingly being developed to equip people with the knowledge needed to navigate an AI-driven world. This trend underscores the importance of fostering a culture of curiosity and understanding around AI, ensuring that everyone, regardless of their background, can engage with and contribute to the ongoing conversation about this transformative technology.

Potential Advancements

The eld of arti cial intelligence is rapidly evolving, and its potential advancements are poised to reshape various aspects of our daily lives. As researchers and industry leaders continue to push the boundaries of what AI can achieve, several key areas stand out as particularly promising. These advancements not only enhance existing technologies but also create new opportunities for innovation across numerous sectors, including healthcare, education, transportation, and entertainment.

One of the most signi cant advancements in AI is the development of more sophisticated machine learning algorithms. These algorithms are designed to analyze vast amounts of data with greater accuracy and ef ciency than ever before. By leveraging deep learning techniques, AI systems can recognize patterns, make predictions, and even generate creative content. This capability has profound implications for industries such as medicine, where AI can assist in diagnosing diseases by analyzing medical images or predicting patient outcomes based on historical data.

Natural language processing (NLP) is another area where AI is making remarkable strides. Advancements in NLP allow machines to understand and generate human language more effectively, leading to improved communication between humans and computers. This technology is already being integrated into virtual assistants, customer service chatbots, and language translation applications. As NLP continues to evolve, we can expect even more intuitive interfaces that facilitate seamless interactions, breaking down language barriers and enhancing accessibility for users around the globe.

Robotics is also on the brink of signi cant transformation through AI advancements. The integration of AI with robotics has the potential to create intelligent machines capable of performing complex tasks in a variety of environments. From autonomous vehicles navigating city streets to drones delivering packages, these innovations promise to enhance ef ciency and safety in transportation. Furthermore, in manufacturing and logistics, AI-powered robots can optimize work ows, reduce human error, and increase productivity, leading to signi cant cost savings and improved operational effectiveness.

Lastly, the ethical considerations surrounding AI development are gaining attention as technology progresses. As AI systems become more capable and autonomous, it is crucial to address issues such as bias, privacy, and accountability. Establishing frameworks for responsible AI development will be essential to ensure that advancements in this eld bene t society as a whole. By fostering collaboration between technologists, ethicists, and policymakers, we can navigate the challenges posed by these advancements and harness the full potential of arti cial intelligence for the greater good.

AI and Job Market Implications

The advent of arti cial intelligence (AI) has been a transformative force across numerous sectors, in uencing how businesses operate and how work is conducted. As AI technologies advance, their implications for the job market become increasingly signi cant. Automation powered by AI is reshaping job descriptions and responsibilities, leading to both opportunities for innovation and challenges regarding workforce displacement. Understanding these dynamics is crucial for anyone navigating the evolving landscape of employment in the age of AI.

AI has the potential to create new job categories that did not previously exist. As companies implement AI systems, there is a growing demand for professionals skilled in AI technologies, data analysis, and machine learning. Roles such as AI ethics compliance of cers, data scientists, and machine learning engineers are emerging as vital components of the modern workforce. This shift highlights the importance of adaptability and continuous learning. Individuals who embrace lifelong learning and seek to acquire new skills relevant to AI will likely nd themselves in a favorable position in the job market.

However, the rise of AI also raises concerns regarding job displacement. Jobs that involve repetitive tasks, such as data entry or routine manufacturing, are particularly vulnerable to automation. This automation can lead to signi cant changes in employment patterns, necessitating a reevaluation of workforce strategies. Governments, educational institutions, and businesses must work collaboratively to ensure that displaced workers are supported through retraining programs and initiatives designed to facilitate transitions into new roles that AI is generating.

Moreover, the integration of AI into various industries can lead to enhanced productivity and ef ciency. By automating mundane tasks, employees can focus on more complex, creative, and strategic aspects of their roles. This shift may enhance job satisfaction and lead to a more engaged workforce. However, it is essential to balance the bene ts of increased productivity with the ethical considerations surrounding AI implementation, including the potential for bias in algorithms and the importance of maintaining human oversight.

In conclusion, the implications of AI on the job market are multifaceted, presenting both opportunities and challenges. As AI continues to evolve, it is imperative for individuals, organizations, and policymakers to stay informed and proactive. Emphasizing education, retraining, and ethical considerations will be crucial in navigating this new landscape. By recognizing the potential of AI while addressing its challenges, society can harness its bene ts to create a more equitable and prosperous future for all workers.

Preparing for an AI-Driven World

As arti cial intelligence continues to permeate various aspects of our lives, it becomes increasingly vital for individuals and organizations to prepare for this transformative shift. Understanding the fundamental principles of AI is the rst step toward navigating its complexities. This includes familiarizing oneself with basic concepts such as machine learning, natural language processing, and data analytics. By gaining a foundational understanding, individuals can make informed decisions about how to leverage AI technologies effectively.

Developing a mindset that embraces change is equally important in an AI-driven world. The rapid evolution of technology necessitates adaptability. Individuals should cultivate a willingness to learn and unlearn as new AI applications emerge. This involves not only staying informed about advancements in AI but also recognizing the potential impact of these technologies on various industries. A proactive approach to learning will empower individuals to harness AI's capabilities rather than be overwhelmed by them.

Collaboration will play a crucial role in successfully integrating AI into everyday life and work. It is essential to foster interdisciplinary communication between technologists, ethicists, and industry leaders. By working together, these groups can address the ethical implications of AI, ensuring that its deployment is responsible and beneficial to society as a whole. Encouraging dialogue around the societal impact of AI will help mitigate potential risks, such as biases in algorithms and job displacement, while maximizing the technology's positive contributions.

Practical experience with AI tools and platforms can significantly enhance one's readiness for an AI-driven future. Engaging with user-friendly AI applications can provide hands-on experience that demystifies the technology. Many free or low-cost resources are available, allowing individuals to explore AI capabilities without requiring an extensive technical background. By experimenting with these tools, one can better appreciate how AI can be applied in various contexts, from automating mundane tasks to enhancing decision-making processes.

Finally, fostering a strong ethical framework is imperative as we prepare for an AI-driven world. This involves understanding the ethical considerations surrounding AI deployment, such as privacy, fairness, and accountability. Individuals and organizations should prioritize transparency and inclusivity in AI development, ensuring that diverse perspectives are represented. By embedding ethical principles into the fabric of AI initiatives, society can work towards a future where technology serves humanity's best interests, ultimately leading to a more equitable and innovative world.

Chapter 8: Getting Started with AI
Learning Resources for Beginners

In the journey of understanding artificial intelligence, having the right resources is crucial for beginners. The landscape of AI can seem overwhelming, filled with complex terminology and advanced concepts. However, a variety of accessible learning materials can effectively bridge the gap between curiosity and comprehension. Books, online courses, tutorials, and community forums serve as essential tools for anyone looking to grasp the fundamentals of AI and its real-world applications.

Books remain one of the most reliable sources for foundational knowledge. Numerous titles cater specifically to beginners, breaking down intricate concepts into digestible sections. Books such as "Artificial Intelligence: A Guide to Intelligent Systems" and "AI Superpowers" provide not only theoretical frameworks but also practical insights into how AI is shaping industries today. These resources often include case studies that illustrate AI's impact, making it easier for novices to relate the content to real-world scenarios.

Online courses have revolutionized how individuals learn about AI. Platforms like Coursera, edX, and Udacity offer structured programs led by experts in the field. These courses typically include video lectures, quizzes, and hands-on projects, catering to various learning styles. Beginners can benefit from introductory courses that cover the basics of machine learning, neural networks, and data analysis, allowing them to progress at their own pace while gaining practical skills. Additionally, many of these platforms provide certifications that can enhance a learner's professional profile.

Tutorials and coding exercises available on websites like Codecademy and Kaggle are invaluable for those who prefer a more interactive approach. These resources often provide step-by-step guidance through coding exercises, allowing learners to apply their knowledge in real-time. Engaging with practical coding challenges not only solidifies theoretical understanding but also builds confidence in using AI tools and programming languages like Python and R, which are essential for any aspiring AI practitioner.

Finally, community forums and social media groups offer a supportive environment for beginners to ask questions, share insights, and collaborate on projects. Platforms such as Reddit, Stack Overflow, and specialized Facebook groups connect learners with experienced professionals and fellow novices alike. Engaging in discussions and seeking advice from seasoned practitioners can greatly enhance a beginner's understanding and provide valuable networking opportunities. By leveraging these diverse learning resources, anyone can embark on a fulfilling journey into the world of artificial intelligence, equipped with the knowledge and skills to navigate its complexities.

Online Courses and Certifications

Online courses and certifications have become pivotal in the education landscape, particularly in the realm of artificial intelligence. With the rapid advancements in AI technologies and their increasing integration into various industries, many individuals seek to enhance their understanding and skills in this field. Online platforms offer a diverse range of courses, catering to different levels of expertise, from complete beginners to those looking to deepen their existing knowledge. These courses are designed to be accessible to everyone, making AI education more inclusive than ever before.

The flexibility of online learning allows individuals to study at their own pace and convenience, which is particularly beneficial for those balancing work or personal commitments. Most online courses offer a mix of video lectures, interactive quizzes, and hands-on projects that enable learners to apply theoretical concepts in practical scenarios. This hands-on approach is crucial in the field of AI, where practical experience is often as important as theoretical knowledge. Furthermore, many platforms provide community forums where students can engage with peers and instructors, fostering a collaborative learning environment.

Certifications from reputable online courses have gained recognition among employers, signaling a candidate's commitment to professional development and their proficiency in AI fundamentals. These credentials can significantly enhance one's resume, providing a competitive edge in the job market. Many companies actively seek individuals with verified skills in AI technologies, and having a certification can demonstrate an individual's dedication to mastering the subject. As industries increasingly adopt AI solutions, the demand for skilled professionals continues to rise, making certifications a valuable asset.

When choosing an online course or certification program, it is essential for learners to consider the course content, the credibility of the issuing institution, and the level of support provided. Many reputable platforms partner with leading universities and organizations to deliver high-quality educational content. It is also advisable to look for courses that offer practical projects or case studies, as these components can greatly enhance understanding and retention of the material. Additionally, reading reviews or testimonials from past participants can provide insights into the course's effectiveness and relevance.

In conclusion, online courses and certi cations serve as powerful tools for anyone looking to understand arti cial intelligence and its real-world applications. They provide an accessible pathway for learners to gain knowledge, develop skills, and enhance their career prospects in a rapidly evolving eld. As AI continues to shape the future of various industries, investing in education through online platforms can empower individuals to navigate this technological landscape with con dence and competence.

Building Your First AI Project

Building your rst AI project can be an exhilarating experience, and it is an essential step in understanding the practical applications of arti cial intelligence. To embark on this journey, you must rst identify a problem that you are passionate about solving. This could range from automating simple tasks, such as data entry, to more complex issues like predicting trends in market behavior. The key is to select a project that aligns with your interests and offers an opportunity to learn while making a tangible impact. By focusing on a speci c challenge, you can maintain motivation and ensure that your efforts are directed toward meaningful results.

Once you have de ned your project, the next step is to gather the necessary data. Data is the foundation of any AI system, and its quality can signi cantly in uence the outcomes of your project. Depending on your chosen problem, you may need to collect data from various sources or utilize publicly available datasets. It is crucial to ensure that the data is relevant, accurate, and representative of the task at hand. Additionally, you should consider the ethical implications of using this data, including privacy concerns and the potential for bias, as these factors can affect the integrity of your AI model.

After gathering the data, the process of data preprocessing begins. This involves cleaning the data, handling missing values, and transforming it into a format suitable for analysis. Preprocessing is often a critical and time-consuming step in AI projects, as the quality of your data directly impacts the performance of your model. Techniques such as normalization, encoding categorical variables, and feature selection can enhance the effectiveness of your AI algorithms. Taking the time to thoroughly preprocess your data can lead to more accurate predictions and insights, ultimately making your project more successful.

At this stage, you can begin selecting and implementing the appropriate AI algorithms. Depending on your project's goals, you might explore options such as supervised learning, unsupervised learning, or reinforcement learning. Tools and frameworks like TensorFlow, PyTorch, or Scikit-learn can facilitate the development of your AI model. As you experiment with different algorithms, it is essential to evaluate their performance using metrics that are relevant to your specic problem. This iterative process of training, testing, and rening your model will help you achieve optimal results.

Finally, once you have built and validated your AI model, it is time to deploy it in a real-world setting. This can involve integrating your model into a user-friendly application or presenting your ndings to stakeholders. Deployment not only showcases your work but also provides an opportunity to gather feedback and iterate further. Remember that the journey does not end with deployment; continuous monitoring and improvement are necessary to adapt to changing conditions and maintain the relevance of your AI solution. By following these steps, you will not only complete your rst AI project but also gain invaluable skills and insights that will serve you well in your future endeavors in the eld of articial intelligence.

Community and Networking in AI

Community and networking play a crucial role in the advancement of articial intelligence, particularly for those just starting their journey in this dynamic eld. Engaging with a community of like-minded individuals provides invaluable opportunities for learning, sharing knowledge, and staying updated with the latest developments in AI. These communities often encompass a diverse range of participants, from beginners to seasoned professionals, creating an environment where everyone can contribute and benet from collective experiences.

Online platforms have emerged as pivotal spaces for AI enthusiasts to connect. Social media groups, forums, and specialized websites foster discussions on various AI topics, allowing participants to ask questions, seek advice, and share insights. Resources such as GitHub enable collaborative projects, where individuals can contribute to open-source AI initiatives. This collaborative spirit not only enhances individual learning but also propels the overall growth of the AI eld, as shared projects can lead to innovative solutions and advancements.

In-person events, such as workshops, conferences, and meetups, also play a signi cant role in building community and networking in AI. These gatherings provide opportunities for participants to engage directly with industry experts, attend lectures, and participate in hands-on sessions. Networking at such events can lead to mentorship opportunities, job prospects, and collaborations that might not be possible in an online setting. Moreover, the chance to interact face-to-face fosters deeper connections and a sense of belonging among participants, which can be particularly motivating for those new to the eld.

Educational institutions and organizations often facilitate community-building efforts through dedicated AI clubs or study groups. These initiatives create a structured environment for learning and collaboration, where members can explore AI concepts together, work on projects, and gain access to resources and mentorship. Such environments are especially bene cial for beginners, as they provide a supportive atmosphere to ask questions and experiment without the fear of judgment, ultimately enhancing their understanding of AI.

As the AI landscape continues to evolve, the importance of community and networking will only grow. For beginners, actively participating in these networks can signi cantly accelerate their learning curve and provide essential support as they navigate the complexities of arti cial intelligence. By leveraging the collective wisdom and resources of the community, individuals can better equip themselves to contribute meaningfully to the eld and stay informed about the latest trends and technologies shaping the future of AI.

Chapter 9: Conclusion
Recap of Key Concepts

The exploration of arti cial intelligence begins with a fundamental understanding of what AI is and its various branches. At its core, arti cial intelligence refers to the simulation of human intelligence processes by machines, particularly computer systems. These processes include learning, reasoning, problem-solving, perception, and language understanding. The distinction between narrow AI, which is designed for speci c tasks, and general AI, which aims to perform any intellectual task that a human can, is crucial for grasping the current capabilities and limitations of AI technologies.

Another key concept is machine learning, a subset of AI that focuses on the development of algorithms that enable computers to learn from and make predictions based on data. Machine learning can be categorized into supervised, unsupervised, and reinforcement learning. Supervised learning requires labeled data to train models, unsupervised learning identi es patterns in unlabeled data, and reinforcement learning involves algorithms that learn by interacting with their environment, receiving feedback based on their actions. Understanding these categories helps clarify how AI systems are trained and how they improve over time.

Deep learning, a further specialization within machine learning, employs neural networks with many layers to analyze various types of data. This approach has revolutionized elds such as image and speech recognition, allowing machines to achieve remarkable accuracy in tasks previously thought to require human intelligence. The principles of deep learning highlight the importance of data quality and quantity, as well as the computational power necessary for training deep neural networks. Recognizing these factors is essential for anyone looking to understand the practical applications of AI in the real world.

In addition to technical concepts, ethical considerations surrounding AI play a vital role in discussions about its future. Issues such as bias in AI algorithms, privacy concerns, and the potential for job displacement due to automation must be critically examined. It is essential for developers, policymakers, and the public to engage in conversations about the responsible deployment of AI technologies. Understanding these ethical dimensions ensures that AI is developed and used in ways that bene t society as a whole, rather than exacerbate existing inequalities.

Finally, the potential applications of AI span multiple industries, from healthcare and nance to transportation and entertainment. AI technologies are already transforming how we approach problem-solving and decision-making, enhancing ef ciency and accuracy in various sectors. As AI continues to evolve, its integration into daily life will likely deepen, making it increasingly important for individuals to stay informed about its developments. A comprehensive grasp of these key concepts equips readers to navigate the complexities of AI and its implications for the future.

The Ongoing Journey of Learning AI

The journey of learning arti cial intelligence is an ongoing process that re ects not only the rapid advancements in technology but also the evolving understanding of what AI can achieve. For beginners, the initial steps into the realm of AI may seem daunting, lled with complex terminologies and intricate theories. However, this journey is accessible to all, regardless of background or expertise. With the right resources and mindset, anyone can embark on this path, paving the way for a deeper comprehension of how AI in uences various aspects of our lives.

As one begins to explore AI, it is essential to grasp the foundational concepts that underpin this eld. Understanding the difference between machine learning, deep learning, and traditional programming is crucial. Each of these components plays a unique role in the development of intelligent systems. Beginners should focus on grasping basic principles, such as algorithms, data sets, and model training. Resources such as online courses, workshops, and community forums offer valuable opportunities to learn from experts and peers, fostering a collaborative environment that enhances understanding.

The importance of practical experience cannot be understated in the learning journey. Engaging in hands-on projects allows beginners to apply theoretical knowledge to real-world scenarios. Whether it involves building simple predictive models or experimenting with AI-powered applications, practical engagement helps solidify concepts and encourages critical thinking. Additionally, participating in hackathons or collaborative projects can expose learners to diverse perspectives and innovative solutions, enriching their understanding of AI's capabilities and limitations.

Continuous learning is paramount in the eld of AI, as technology and methodologies evolve at a breakneck pace. Staying updated with the latest research, trends, and tools is essential for anyone looking to deepen their knowledge. Subscribing to relevant journals, attending conferences, and joining online communities can provide insights into current advancements and best practices. This commitment to lifelong learning not only enhances one's technical skills but also cultivates a mindset that is adaptable and forward-thinking.

Finally, the journey of learning AI is not solely about mastering technical skills; it also involves ethical considerations and societal impacts. As AI systems are increasingly integrated into everyday life, understanding the ethical implications of these technologies becomes crucial. Beginners should reflect on questions of bias, privacy, and accountability in AI applications. By fostering a holistic understanding of AI that encompasses both its technical and ethical dimensions, learners can contribute to the responsible development and application of artificial intelligence, ensuring that it serves the greater good in society.

Embracing AI in Everyday Life

Embracing AI in everyday life signifies a transformative shift in how individuals interact with technology, enhancing efficiency and convenience across various aspects of daily activities. From personal assistants like Siri and Alexa to recommendation algorithms on streaming services, AI is woven into the fabric of modern living. These applications not only streamline tasks but also adapt to individual preferences, making technology more intuitive and user- friendly. Understanding the role of AI in these everyday tools is essential for harnessing their full potential and appreciating the advancements they bring to our routines.

One of the most significant areas where AI has made a profound impact is in communication. Smart messaging apps now utilize AI to enhance user experience through features such as predictive text and automated responses. These innovations save time and reduce the cognitive load on users, allowing for more efficient interactions. Furthermore, AI-driven translation tools break down language barriers, enabling seamless communication among people from diverse linguistic backgrounds. As these technologies continue to evolve, they promise to foster greater connectivity and understanding in an increasingly globalized world.

In the realm of healthcare, AI is revolutionizing the way individuals manage their health and wellness. Wearable devices equipped with AI algorithms monitor vital signs, track physical activity, and even predict potential health risks based on user data. This proactive approach to health management empowers individuals to make informed decisions about their well-being. Additionally, AI-driven telemedicine platforms facilitate remote consultations, making healthcare more accessible to those in remote or underserved areas. These advancements not only enhance individual health outcomes but also contribute to a more efficient healthcare system overall.

The integration of AI in nancial services is another area where its bene ts are becoming increasingly apparent. Personal nance applications utilize AI to analyze spending habits, provide budgeting recommendations, and even detect fraudulent activities in real-time. This level of insight allows users to take control of their nances, making informed decisions that align with their nancial goals. Furthermore, AI is pivotal in streamlining processes such as loan approvals and investment strategies, democratizing access to nancial resources and advice that were once limited to traditional institutions.

Finally, the incorporation of AI in home automation is reshaping how individuals interact with their living spaces. Smart home devices, powered by AI, learn user preferences and adjust settings for lighting, temperature, and security accordingly. This level of customization not only enhances comfort but also promotes energy ef ciency and safety. As more households adopt these technologies, the concept of a connected home becomes increasingly mainstream, paving the way for smarter and more responsive living environments. Embracing AI in everyday life is not just about adopting new technologies; it is about recognizing the potential for positive change in how we live and interact with the world around us.

www.ingramcontent.com/pod-product-compliance
Lightning Source LLC
LaVergne TN
LVHW060125070326
832902LV00019B/3138